dear girl: *a reckoning*

Book design : *Cindi Kusuda*

Published : *Gold Line Press*

http://goldlinepress.com

Gold Line titles are distributed by Small Press Distributions

This title is also available for purchase directly from the publisher

www.spdbooks.org : 800.869.7553

Library of Congress Cataloging-in-Publication Data

dear girl : *drea brown*

Library of Congress Control Number 2015942420

brown, drea

ISBN 978-1-938900-15-0

FIRST EDITION

dear girl

a reckoning

drea brown

dear reader

believe me when i tell you i am haunted

by marvelous horrors of past-not-passed

tenebrous and fleshly thunderous things

don't you believe in ghosts   this lineage

of banshees and haints tongue-snatched

or conch ears manacled neck   overboard

or below deck thick in blood memory

inherited apparitions some come to stay

awhile here is the reckoning   believe

me reader the dead will have their due

dream in which the girl takes shape

eyes become eyes in the dark

a body begins silhouettes

against moon-skin

smaller than i imagined

fine-lined frame one thin arm

reaches out raises a briny finger

points   as though i am accused

or something she chooses

you

you

you

how to explain the mark it left

indelible memory

finger poised like drying ink

sonnet /conjure: tongue untie

what to do with the bitters of all that is seen in sleep

wrapped in muslin and straw   so many years topsy-turvy

dolled in bales of memory   a tongue grows weary of murmur

swells like tubers yearns to pop fetters bust through seams

say yours is waterlogged mother-marked welled with grief

chart voice across atlantic   harbor geographic tongue-tears

watery stanchion pulpy oyster how to emancipate an organ

wrung with passage and piety may there be mercy

molasses for suture dear girl remember your name

the way your mama smells melon to cool libation at dawn

salt water baby's breath rum for virility of epiglottal pearl

what to do with the liquor of dreams what is there to say

lilt a litany let me smudge sweet grass for feather tongue

let me search currents for comfort mouth wide to return girl

DEAR
GIRL

16

cross-
section
of the
schooner
phillis[1]

deck-deck-deck-deck-deck-deck-deck-deck-deck-deck-deck-deck-deck-deck-deck

bodybodybodybodybodybodybodybodybodybodybodybodybodybodybodybo

bodybodybodybodybodybodybodybodybodybodybodybodybodybodybodybo

bodybodybodybodybodybodybodybodybodybodybodybodybodybodybodybo

bodybodybodybodybodybodybodybodybodybodybodybodybodybodybodybo

bodybodybodybodybodybodybodybodybodybodybodybodybodybodybodybo

barrels of molasses casks of rum sugar gunpowder barrels of molasses casks of rum

barrels of molasses casks of rum sugar gunpowder barrels of molasses casks of rum

barrels of potatoes bushels of onion barrels barrels of potatoes bushels of onion b

loaves of sugar barrels of potatoes loaves of sugar barrels of potatoes bushels of o

casks of rum snuff pickled mackerel loaves casks of rum snuff pickled mackerel loa

casks of rum snuff pickled mackerel loaves casks of rum snuff pickled mackerel loa

pine oars musket balls axes turpentine tire iron pine oars musket balls axes turper

pine oars musket balls axes turpentine tire iron pine oars musket balls axes turper

pistols musket balls cutlass gun flints hank pistols musket balls cutlass gun flints ha

handkerchiefs sheathing boards pitch handkerchiefs sheathing boards pitch

cabin stools powder tobacco cabin stools powder tobacco

```
          over      indigo          waves    rushing          ebbing

     and         oyster    and          angel fish        bodies sink

                                under  water           black  cold

          indigo                      angels   slip                      fle


black              fish         black       fish                     blac
```

over

ck-deck-deck-deck-deck-deck-deck

odybodybodybodybodybodybody

odybodybodybodybodybodybody

rlbodybodybodybodybodybodyb

odybodybodybodybodybodybod   over

odybodybodybodybodybodybo

vder white bread barrels of me

gunpowder white bread bar   over

  pickled mackerel loaves

rels of pickled macke

gar coffee me

gar coffee

  iron pi   over

  ir

                                    splash
                        over
              splash   sinking   black   splash   blacks   sink

h tide   over   waves   rush   indigo   high tide

black   and bone   indigo   waves rush

  sink in angel   bodies   soak   or   swim
                                                   sink

      rushing   s e a

                                                      no   swim

      fish   s e e

begin again   here where water

funnels and purls against slaver

bowels swirls over sharks' patient

teeth   here or there where bodies

are force fitted into cargo and coffin

space   begin with cowrie with trade

gold coast goree bight of benin

begin and do not cannot go back

say coffle noose neck babble

branding by fire iron livestock

severed   forgotten no more

bop: passage in simile [2]

bop passage

like when a body cannot see

itself beginning again

anywhere   but in pillows

of sea foam shards of sea glass

lashing obsidian troubled flesh

so it/he/she/they jump

waves and waves on waves

like mothers whose faces become

indigo ripples jade and turquoise

beneath leaps and splashes

shoveling ocean into mouths

like mashed yam

spools of tides and salt

like olokun reaching past coral

mausoleums toward yemoja's skirts

waves   and waves   on waves   devolving

blues and breath and sea ash

glittering hems miniscule shells

rattling current like

handfuls of molars or bone

like moon waxing gibbous luminous

witness heavy-eyed hanged in grief

and waves and waves on waves

devolving without end

when bodies are unable to mourn

traumatic situations   the memory

is stored in a secret place to touch

later or not at all   if these things

remain locked a haunting occurs

consider the girl who in her angelic

script was unable to say all that

was tucked away   i implore you

too much has already been lost

there is always already urgency

to piece in place what has not

been said   i am talking about

scouring in graves   plunging

in hopes something will float[3]

for days and days

all these bodies   gleaming flesh   mute muscle   locked ankles   all this filth
this puss this blood this black this wail   this one dies   two hundred forty
days   this deck   this dance   this girl   she would not eat   this black these
bodies   that lash   her back split open   she died and another another
one gave birth to blood and more blood she died   and another another
and i think   what is my name   two hundred forty days and there is no air
down here just dark and stench and vomit and   sometimes one girl holds
her breath   she draws the ocean on my back   waves and fish one day
she jumps   a feast for sharks they thrash we dance and scrub what is left
this fat belly of wood   this world and where we   where we going   this
black below   and one night after music   the landsman come   he check the
chains   he let mine loose   these wrists this raw   my legs stumble on deck
it is too dark to dance this night this moon this man give me sugar no
horse bean no mash this man give me sugar i watch the moon   his hands
these bodies this dark his hands this sweet this night this blue black blue
this moon   sugar is the color of moon this land float his hands one day
i will become the moon   two hundred forty days i get tongue burn and

sour teeth   i don't die but a woman do she become a bird   then splash

and all these bodies these all this sun this sun this two hundred forty days

and another and another another and one night when my mouth stinging

sweet i see my ma smile underwater i think of the moon   watch her smile

turn to black and blue eye wink watch she grow a tail and glow my ma

she is the sea i think two hundred forty days i think my ma is the sea and

i want to be the moon or a pearl breathe underwater there is no air here

in this dark just we sick and die and moan   more bodies turn into black

birds fish free and my mama in the sea where we   how many days now

reader this is my hope that in voyage across

churning waters in the filth and

forgotten self there were moments of warmth

and benevolence bodies

connected beyond flesh if only for two

hundred and forty days restored a sense of self

and life for a moment reader allow me to reach

further into the water to find something akin to

mercy or salvation

these things i believe

mercy visits the schooner phillis

twas mercy brought me from my pagan land[4]

had i come another time girl

      you would already be gone

stored above

tobacco and casks of rum

one body becoming

another

and another

another

rows of ashen marrow

fastened with puss and pox

      you are already a miracle

for now

i am all the body needed

to keep you breathing

thunderheads and pearl

shimmer and tail flick

bone taster salt sting

moon blood iridescent

remember me as dream

in one

      you are born

with cowries in your mouth

in another you are a fish

bathed indigo and myrrh

i water your tongue

teach it to master itself

      you will wake

bridled and born again

nothing will be your own

they will claim and call you

many things

      remember

you are a miracle

fix your lips like this girl

say it

begin again two hundred and forty days

twenty-one deaths how many floggings

how many hands how many moons

how long this ache and pulse in her teeth

come to this country tongue-snatched and

barely breathing come weary-eyed wary

of land and what should she become next

girl on the deck of terror and wonder[5]

was kidnapped

       forced to cross atlantic

face land in boston

the child

the phillis   brought

sold small   little value   called:

refuse   gift   commodity

renamed:

slaveship   improbable   mother

america's

phillis land-ho! cleaned and oiled and fed black and shining like a premonition or phenomenon. phillis primed for sale gawked at and prodded and squeezed. what did she know? what death? whose hands? phillis in boston, phillis purchased, phillis named after sarcophagus at sea. whose idea was that? why that? lest she forgot from where she came? lest she begin to think herself more than cargo and chattel, because who has time to really think of names for such things? phillis whose name meant slave and sounded like sorrow song. nothing about her was her own. name body tongue god. how to become this new thing when you have already learned you are human?

the girl for prod and purchase

was it a nice day? does it matter?[6]

let us say a finger is put to your mouth

chafed lips cracking beneath the touch

let us say too it finds a way in examines

cheek to inside cheek   becomes a hand

pries the cotton mouth weighs down on tongue

say the tongue is coated in summer salt and liquor

say you nod indifferently as a man speaks

raises the bony length of your arm

knocks on your right knee

thigh slaps

turn around

back pat

what happens when fingers move to teeth

the length of them fattening across a gummy space

does your jaw ache does it tremble

so all that can be done is to suck a bit

pray for sugar

or girl do you bite

rememory: on sea monsters mermaids and salvation

I.

the monsters came pocked and red-cheeked

strings limping from their heads to the base

of their sickly white necks

they sliced through mama's body

in wooden worlds named for phantom women

and incomprehensible things

i am called one of these

phillis

the others will haunt me until i am a ghost

but i smile and position my body as taught

susannah

sarah

jesus

mercy

2.

see how i do pretty things

make letters into lace

the dead into elegy and sweet cream

i click my tongue quietly

for the sake of history

spit before i speaking

it is the only way to mind

what comes out

3.

once while on deck

i thought i saw a school of glowing fish

the lot of them synchronized in swim

but i was wrong it was always mama

her eyes lit against slick oils of ocean

now i search out blues so i will not forget:

robin egg ribbon juniper berry

roll my tongue against the back of my teeth

i spit

and write

jesus saves

rememory: questions after transit

q: do you remember your first storm over water?

a: only that the air was dank with dying

the sound of water knocking and

praying dying praying

and sobbing my own?

q: because you were alone?

a: because

i could see

my mother's face

q: and did she speak?

a: only murmurs

her voice already underwater

q: but did you touch her?

a: i must have

i woke soaked in salt

the dead will have their due. they will speak from graves or whisper into the ears of poets who search oceans, to begin here with rupture or capture or loss. we are a haunted people, defined by crags of history and silence that have only increased the pang and swell in phantom limbs of cultural memory. by excavating tombs of historical trauma by querying what the body or spirit stores and aches to release, we can reckon with the haunt and give voice to what is sunken or buried.

NOTES

1

Biographer Vincent Carretta notes that "although it is impossible to identify exactly where Wheatley's journey from Africa to America began, some commentators have asserted […] she was born in Senegal. Others say Gambia." She was kidnapped in 1761 during the transatlantic slave trade and brought to Boston for purchase aboard the schooner *Phillis*, for which she was later named. See Vincent Carretta's *Phillis Wheatley: Biography of a Genius in Bondage* (Athens, GA: Univ. of Georgia Press, 2011), pg. 9.

2

Refrain taken from line 26 of Wheatley's poem "Ocean" from *Complete Writings*, edited by Vincent Carretta (New York: Penguin, 2001), pg. 78.

In Yoruba cosmologies, Yemoja and Olokun are Orishas or divinities found in oceans and salt waters. Yemoja is a fierce and loving mother-protector of children and womb, her fingers rippling every living thing in the sea. Olokun rules the watery mysteries of the deep, the dead and imagined possibilities. As these religions spread during Middle Passage, the calls and beliefs of the Orisha crossed as well.

3

Much of my thought process in working through these pieces draws from my research on haunting and inheritance, particularly Nicolas Abraham and Maria Torok's work on transgenerational haunting and Avery Gordon's sociological exploration *Ghostly Matters*.

4

Epigraph taken from the first line of Wheatley's poem "On Being Brought
From Africa to America" from *Complete Writings*, edited by Vincent Carretta
(New York: Penguin, 2001), pg. 13.

5

This is an erasure piece. All text is taken from page 1 of chapter 1, "On Being
Brought from Africa to America," of Vincent Carretta's biography of
Wheatley, *Phillis Wheatley: Biography of a Genius in Bondage* (Athens, GA: Univ.
of Georgia Press, 2011).

6

From June Jordan's "The Difficult Miracle of Black Poetry in America" in *Some
of Us Did Not Die: New and Selected Essays of June Jordan* (New York: Basic/Civi-
tas, 2002), pg. 174-86.

7

Toni Morrison coins this term in her novel *Beloved* as a means of revisiting and/
or reliving memory, whether physically or mentally. Often, a rememory tugs on
the senses. Rememory, similar to Adrienne Rich's re-membering, calls for fresh
eyes on the past–a restructuring and re-imagining.

drea brown's work has appeared in a variety of literary journals and anthologies, most recently *Southern Indiana Review* and *Stand Our Ground: Poems for Trayvon Martin and Marissa Alexander*. A Cave Canem Fellow, drea currently lives in Austin and is a PhD candidate in Black Studies at the University of Texas.